TEACHER'S LITTLE BOOK OF WISDOM

A Couple Hundred Suggestions, Observations and Reminders for Teachers to Read, Remember and Share.

By Bob Algozzine

ICS BOOKS, Inc.
Merrillville, IN

Teacher's Little Book of Wisdom

Copyright © 1995 by Bob Algozzine.

10 9 8 7 6 5 4 3 2 1

All rights reserved, including the right to reproduce this book or portions thereof
in any form or by any means, electronic or mechanical, including photocopying,
recording, unless authorization is obtained, in writing, from the publisher.

All inquiries should be addressed to ICS Books, Inc, 1370 E. 86th Place, Merrillville, IN 46410

Published by:
ICS BOOKS, Inc
1370 E. 86th Place
Merrillville, IN 46410
800-541-7323

Printed in the U.S.A.
All ICS titles are printed on 50% recycled paper from
pre-consumer waste. All sheets are processed without
using acid.

Library of Congress Cataloging-in-Publication Data

Algozzine, Robert
    Teacher's little book of wisdom / by Bob Algozzine.
        p.   cm.
    ISBN 1-57034-017-X
    1. Teachers -- Miscellanea. 2. Teaching -- Miscellanea. I. Title.
LB1775 . A417 1995
371 . 1' 02--dc20   95-15940
                                                      CIP

Dedication

To Kate, whose love and wisdom helped make teaching
Kathryn and Mike a limitless joy, comfort, and success and whose
teaching continues to give wisdom and joy to me and
the people she teaches.

Preface

Children should be seen not heard.
Teaching is serious work.
Don't smile until Christmas.
Some of the deepest truths I know came from children.
School should be fun.
Never eat anything in the lunchroom covered completely with brown gravy.

These are some kernels of wisdom (and how I translated some others) that I took from an early education course. With a bachelor's degree in economics, one does not receive much wisdom about teaching. One often does not become a teacher (especially a special education teacher) with a bachelor's degree in economics. But, now and then, if one is very lucky, an opportunity arises that can change your life. I started teaching with no education for it. I started teaching with insecurity greater than the content void created by being an undergraduate, non-education major. Now, a few years later, I am a very good teacher (or so I have been told) and many whom I have taught are pretty good at it too. This book reflects some of what (a.k.a, the wisdom) I learned from spending my adult life teaching.

The wisdom in this book was collected from many sources. Some of it is based on research, though I hope you won't know it from the way I have tried to disguise it. I am thankful to my professional colleagues who reached conclusions that I could convert to wisdom to be passed along in a book like this rather than in a textbook you might be forced to read. Some of it is based on messages I have seen or heard in other places. I am thankful to friends and strangers who provided "food for thought" to be converted to wisdom in a book like this. Some of it just came to me in the middle of the night. I am thankful that I had a piece of paper and a pen to write it down for a book like this.

Nothing in this book was intended to change your life. If something makes you smile, makes you laugh, makes you trust what you are doing in your class or with your students, or makes you think about teaching in a positive way, I'll be happy. Actually, I'll be happy without it, but it doesn't hurt to hope that something you have done might make a difference in the life of somebody else. And, that's a teacher's dream.

P.S. Enjoy the book.

Bob Algozzine

1. Dream big dreams but be known for what you do.

2. Teach so that when your students think of fun, joy, and learning, they think of you.

3. Show respect to children and youth.

4.   Surprise your students with unexpected
       gifts.

5.   Believe your students want to learn
       something new every day.

6.   If you make mistakes, try not to make
       them again.

7.   Never force anyone to do anything.

8.   Teach your students to tell the principal how much they enjoy being in your class.

9.   Remember you can weigh manure with a jeweler's scale and slice baloney with a laser beam, but when you're done you still have manure and baloney.

10.   Teach something that's not part of the curriculum.

11.   Have a field trip every day (write to me for ideas).

12.   At least once a month, toss out your plans and do what you like.

13.   When playing games with children, let them win more than once in a while.

14. Strive for doing things right, not just doing the right things.

15. Avoid being negative.

16. Treat the people you teach like you want to be treated.

17. Teach them it is better to shoot for the stars and miss than to aim for a pile of manure and hit it.

18. Don't be afraid to make mistakes but be sure to learn from them.

19. Encourage children to be curious. When they say it can't be done, ask, "Why not?"

20. Encourage children to ask, "Why?" and "Why not?" a lot.

21. Bring a treat to school for your colleagues once a year – bring a treat to your class one a month.

22. Teach your students not to suffer from delusions of adequacy.

23. Encourage every child to be an expert at something.

24. Set high expectations and hold children to them.

25. Set high expectations and hold yourself to them.

26. Teach by this adage: You don't have to be sick to get better.

27. Spend time fixing problems, not fixing blame.

28. Don't talk about your students unless you have something good to say.

29. Be a good listener.

30. Be a good speaker.

31. Get help when you need it.

32. Spend less time figuring out what's wrong and more time doing things right.

33. Avoid paralysis by analysis.

34. Praise someone every week. Praise your students every day.

35. Avoid looking tired or depressed.

36. Be frank – when somebody bugs you let them know nicely.

37.   Remember, advice is often
      free and too often we get
      what we pay for.

38.   Keep records of things that work.

39.   Use great assignments over and over again.

40.   Always deliver more than you promise.

41.   Lose a battle if it will help win a war.

42.   Don't judge a book by its cover.

43.   Point out the good in your students.

44. Respect experience and be sure your children have some.

45. Look for opportunities to tell students how much they mean to you.

46. Take a ride on a school bus to understand how some children start and end the school day.

47. Keep children busy.

48. Let students correct their own work, but be sure to verify performance.

49. Be cheerful, even when you don't feel like it.

50. Be enthusiastic, even when you don't feel like it.

51. Treat children as you would your own.

52. Don't worry. Be happy.

53. Let children be smarter
than you are.

54. Avoid being dull.

55. Avoid making simple things complex.

56. Avoid all discussions of whether anal-retentive has a hyphen.

57. Always try to do sensible things for children and youth.

58. Never label a student you can give a name to.

59. Spend time with children outside of school – even if they act as if they don't like it.

60. Value due process but avoid valuing process more than do.

61. Periodically try to forget all that you were taught was right and simply do what you believe is right.

62. Avoid the tendency to find problems. Try to find solutions.

63. Challenge authority, especially your own.

64.   Enjoy children despite how others label them.

65.   Show children how much you love them – first with words, but more with actions.

66.   Don't talk about the parents of your students unless you have wonderful things to say.

67.   Think.

68. Once a week get to work early and leave a little late. Take a picture of your classroom clock and drop it by your principal's office.

69. Have many definitions for "mastery."

70. Strive for perfection but settle for continuing improvement.

71. Take children the way they are but expect them to change.

72. Give your children a favorite book at least once a year.

73. Share cartoons with your colleagues.

74. Share cartoons with your students.

75. Strive for perfection but settle for performance.

76.   Do things even if they don't appreciate them.

77.   Try something new at least once a month.

78. Promise big.
Deliver bigger.

79.   Eat well. Teaching is tough work.

80.   Build bridges, don't burn them.

81.   Use <u>yes</u> and <u>no</u> judiciously.

82. Teach them some content that is above their grade level.

83. Remember, a successful class depends on two things: (1) having students and (2) being a good teacher.

84. See problems as foundations for solutions.

85.   Be cautious in conversations that begin
       with, "Let me be perfectly honest."

86.   Treat them like people if you think
       it will make a difference.

87. Teach them that "life ain't fair."

88. Never leave your classroom a mess. You may be in an accident and then what?

89. Rate your success by many standards.

90. Never nap during an instructional presentation, particularly your own.

91.   Tell your principal what you think of the cafeteria food.

92.   Value the work done by your school's support staff.

93.   Value the work done by your school's custodial staff.

94. Value the work done by your fellow teachers.

95. Value the work you do.

96. Don't criticize them, even if they deserve it.

97. Don't criticize your children's parents – you may be one of them.

98. Send them a postcard when you go on vacation.

99. Look for opportunities to engage in random acts of niceness.

100. Use all the colors of the rainbow.

101. Use all the crayons in the box.

102. Learn to separate diversity from deviance.

103. See things that haven't been and ask why not.

104. Teach your students that a closed fist cannot accept a gift and a closed mind cannot accept ideas.

105. Remember, if you don't do something right, it's just one more way of not doing it.

106. Teach your students to discover wisdom rather than expect you to provide it.

107. Teach your students to wear their learning like a watch and pull it out whenever they need it.

108. Teach your students that life is a play where performance is more important than perfection.

109. Value compassion, discourage obsession.

110. Remember, positive lessons are not always learned in positive ways.

111. Take their pictures often and plaster them all over your classroom.

112. Don't worry about being wrong, just be right more often.

113. Don't be first at school all the time.

114. Don't be last to leave school all the time.

115. Every day look for some small way to improve your teaching.

116. Every now and then, go through a whole day without criticizing anyone.

117. Let them overhear you saying nice things about them to other teachers.

118. To get things done, avoid committees.

119. Use your computer every day.

120. If parents want to give you gifts, ask for books for their children to read.

121. If you "find" some money, buy some books for your class.

122. Know the difference between right and wrong.

123. Start each day with a song, a joke, or a funny story.

124. Have something simple for them to do every time they come back to the classroom (write to me for ideas).

125. Do a day without dittos.

126. Look for a silver lining in
every cloud.

127. Learn how to make lemons into lemonade.

128. Every once in a while get to school a little late.

129. Have unbirthday parties.

130. Be sure every child receives at least one Valentine card.

131. Be enthusiastic about your students' successes.

132. Don't put off until tomorrow what you can do today.

133. Blame success on ability and effort.

134. Read to your children every day.

135. Listen to your children read every day.

136. Create a positive reputation and value it.

137. Don't accept "no" for an answer, unless it is the answer.

138. Treat "can't" as a four-letter word they don't use in your room.

139. Stop, look, and listen.

140. When asking questions, wait at least five seconds for answers.

141. Make a list of twenty things you want to accomplish during the year and refer to it often.

142. Treat them as people who know something you don't; learn from them.

143. Show children you are a person who knows something they don't.

144. Let them see you laugh.

145. Treat them like people and with any luck they will act like them.

146. Don't be afraid to say you don't know the answer.

147. Don't be afraid to ask for help.

148. Don't be afraid to say you made a mistake.

149. Keep a notebook and pencil handy; ideas come at the strangest times.

150. Encourage children to give up an hour of TV for reading or writing about stuff they like.

151. Attend their ball games, plays, and dance recitals.

152. Look for opportunities to make them feel important.

153. Set long-term goals and short-term plans to achieve them.

154. When planning field trips, read about the places you'll visit before you go, or talk to people who have gone, or better yet, go on a trial trip.

155. Teach by example.

156. Avoid assignments that won't be finished.

157. Take them to a good movie.

158. Avoid anything in the lunchroom covered completely with brown gravy.

159. Avoid being tired, angry, or bored at work.

160. Accept them the way they are, not the way you want them to be.

161. Cooperate, communicate, and display mutual respect and trust.

162. Be somebody's best friend.

163. Teach them to identify at least a dozen plants, flowers, and trees.

164. See things that haven't been done
and ask why not.

165. Value diversity.

166. Challenge tradition.

167. At least once a year share a book with a friend (start with this one).

168. Don't teach to the test unless you give the test.

169. Let them read what they like, over and over again.

170. Remember the three most important things in teaching: teaching, teaching, and teaching.

171. Teach them to find the solution, not fix the blame.

172. Teach them that problem-solving is more than problem-finding.

173. Teach that men and women are equal and that other differences among people are trivial and unimportant.

174. Remember, there is no right way to do a wrong thing.

175. Let children's laughter
remind you how
it 'spozed to be.

176. Remember that sometimes all of a little just isn't enough.

177. Be careful the things you say; children will listen.

178. Be careful the things you do; children will see…and learn.

179. Sometimes give them what they
want – not what you think they need.

180. Make somebody smile every day.

181. Never laugh at an answer unless
it was meant to be funny.

182. Accept a breath mint if a student offers you one.

183. Reward good behavior.

184. When things are going well, notify your class.

185. Have a discipline plan in place but use it gently.

186. Keep a record of what you have done during the year and share it with your principal before leaving for summer vacation.

187. Start each day by reading something thoughtful and inspiring.

188. End each day by reading something thoughtful and inspiring.

189. Let them go to the restroom whenever they want as long as they don't get in trouble there.

190. Start a class bank account and put a little in it each week. Use it to buy books at the end of the year.

191. Don't make threats you can't keep.

192. Avoid having small animals in your classroom.

193. Find a place and plant some seasonal flowers around your school.

194. Find a school improvement project for your class.

195. Share your favorite song lyrics with your class.

196. Have them memorize a few good poems.

197. Find a positive word to describe each of them.

198. Don't think elaborate assignments
will make up for good teaching
or practice.

199. Teach the three Rs:
Respect for yourself,
Responsibility for your actions,
and Remembering the rights
of others.

200. Always try to make the punishment fit the crime.

201. When deciding if a punishment fits a crime, ask them what they think is fair.

202. Teach them that you don't accept unacceptable behavior.

203. Don't rule something out until you have the whole story.

204. Teach them to trust each other but protect their valuables.

205. Teach them to keep their private thoughts private.

206. Teach them that nobody has all the answers.

207. Teach them the difference between things that need doing better than they have been done before, things that just need doing, and things that don't need to be done at all.

208. Purchase best-selling books, read them to your class, and then give them away as prizes for good behavior.

209. Teach them the more they know, the less they will have to fear.

210. Encourage them to read more.

211. Encourage them to watch "public television" at least once a week.

212. Teach them that deadlines are important.

213. Teach them to aim before they fire.

214. Teach them to succeed
without bragging.

215. Don't discredit ideas simply because you don't like the producers.

216. Remember, teachers don't make a lot of money but the work enriches the spirit.

217. Teach them to accept the consequences of their behavior.

218. Don't expect them to know what you want if you don't tell them.

219. Have students spend some time working alone each day.

220. Have students spend some time working in groups each day.

221. Pay attention to things that are working and things that are not working well.

222. Plant a tree with your class at least once a year.

223. Look for ways to praise them every day.

224. Adopt a simple community improvement project (e.g., put a trash can in the park, organize a trash collection expedition in the park, donate books to a library) for your class.

225. Be as friendly to the custodian as you are to the principal.

226. Make them read every day.

227. Make them write every day.

228. "Publish" things they have written at least once a year.

229. Strive for a peaceful, loving atmosphere in your classroom.

230. When you ask them to do something, don't follow it with, "Okay?" Instead, ask if they understand, and then say, "Tell me what I want you to do."

231. Teach them to do a good job because they want to, not because they have to.

232. Teach them to be gentle with themselves, their friends, their community, and the environment.

233. Teach them to appreciate what police officers, firefighters, emergency personnel, and teachers do.

234. Make "Joke-Teller" one of your classroom helpers.

235. Tell them not to ride in the back of pickup trucks or to ride their bikes barefooted.

236. Teach them that waiting doesn't make difficult things easier to do.

237. When there's heavy work to do, teach them not to hold the door.

238. Teach them to reject and condemn discrimination based on race, gender, religion, age, life style, or disability.

239. Keep a file of assignments and activities that went really well.

240. Teach them that very small differences sometimes separate "winners" from everybody else.

241. Be more ready than you think you will have to be.

242. Teach them to respect and be courteous around older people.

243. Teach them when to ignore and when to act.

244. Take a field trip using "public transportation."

245. Teach them to answer the easy questions first.

246. Teach them to trust their memory, but "write it down."

247. Celebrate *April Fool's Day* once a month.

248. Every now and then send a letter home telling how proud you are of what they are doing in school.

249. Teach them that rights always carry responsibilities.

250. Every now and then, encourage them to "follow the yellow brick road."

251. Teach them that what's popular isn't always right.

252. Teach them that seven days without reading makes one weak.

253. Teach them not to cry wolf.

254. Teach them to say what they mean and mean what they say.

255. Teach them that some do,
some don't,
and you might.

256. Teach them that small deeds done
      are better than great deeds planned
      and undone.

257. Show them you don't need a
      weatherman to know which way the
      wind blows.

258. Give your students the confidence to go anywhere, but not without a map.

259. If you are trying to do everything right, stop – and start doing things well.

260. Remember, those who hesitate are often last.

261. Learn to allow more time than you think a project will take.

262. Always set realistic goals but don't set them in cement.

263. Make a conscious effort to teach them that perfection is often an unnecessary ideal.

264. Avoid being someone who is impossible to please because you are seldom pleased with yourself.

265. Teach them the best way to have a friend is to be one.

266. Start the day with the most difficult task.

267. Always have backup activities ready.

268. Remember that even though Babe Ruth hit 714 home runs, he struck out more than 1,300 times.

269. Learn how to say no, especially if you hardly ever do it.

270. Remember, even the person who graduates last in the law school class can be a lawyer.

271. Give them permission to make mistakes.

272. Teach them to give and take praise.

273. Be careful not to damn them with faint praise.

274. Remember, reading achievement is highly related to how much time they spend reading in and out of school – and too often they spend too little.

275. Remember, performance is more effort and commitment than innate ability.

276. Ask questions that require students to do more than recall simple facts.

277. Ask questions that require students to apply what they are learning.

278. Ask questions that require students to analyze what they are learning.

279. Ask questions that require students to synthesize what they are learning.

280. Ask questions that require students to evaluate what they are learning.

281. Be sure homework assignments directly relate to classwork.

282. Monitor performance and progress — frequently and systematically.

283. Always relate new content to subject matter that has already been taught.

284. Remember that good character is fostered by surrounding students with good characters.

285. Teach them to value and use their libraries.

286. Support the arts.

287. If students leave your room for special classes, take time to ensure that lessons in both classes are coordinated.

288. Always be open to any suggestions for improving what and how you teach.

289. Teach them that the best way to learn anything is to start early and study intensively.

290. Teach them to be kind to animals.

291. Take some time at the end of every day to share something positive with each of them.

292. Don't go outside on rainy days.

293. When you ask your principal for something and don't get it, let parents ask the next time, and let children ask the last time.

294. Some of them will be good at lots of things and some of them will be good at only a few – making all of them good at more is some of the fun of teaching.

295. Start with good questions and hopefully good answers will follow.

296. Every class has a top, middle, and bottom – don't let this control how you teach.

297. Make sure they all leave your class good at something.

298. Make ripples more than waves.

299. Always take your keys when you leave your room (even for a minute) with children in it.

300. Remember, all shades of gray come from black and white.

301. Remind your students often that Edison tried thousands of different materials before settling on carbon filament for light bulbs.

302. Show your students how they can travel more than 10,000 miles and still stay where they are.

303. Don't blame the mirror if your face looks angry or unhappy.

304. Push the envelope of quality – there really are no boundaries on how good you can be.

305. Don't miss the forest for the trees.

306. Teach them to follow their dreams and enjoy the trip.

307. Try to cast a spell past what you can see.

308. Try to be the dream, not the destination.

309. Help them get over the loss each time they lose.

310. Show them how to be a hero, not just blame one.

311. Take chances every chance you get.

312. Teach them to work without a net, at least every now and then.

313. Try to use only what you need.

314. Try to have only what you need.

315. Remember that sometimes the more you find out, the less you know.

316. Teach them that actions speak louder than words.

317. Show them that sometimes you get there faster by turning back.

318. Help them see that it's not how smart you are but how you are smart that really makes the difference.

319. Try to fix it long before it is broken.

320. Take them anywhere, but don't abandon them there.

321. Teach them to measure twice and cut once.

322. Teach them there is no failure, only feedback.

323. Remember, you probably won't change anybody's life by improving their self concept, but surely it can't hurt.

324. Show them an ounce of prevention is worth a pound of cure.

325. Show them an ounce of pretension is worth a pound of manure.

326. Show them an ounce of intervention is worth a pound of assure.

327. Teach them that quality often comes in small doses but wears very well.

328. Remember, if you teach a pig to dance, he might not like it.

329. Make allowances for their weakness for the sake of their virtues.

330. Remember, the benefits of knowing often lie in knowing what you don't know.

331. Show your students the wisdom of picking battles that are big enough to matter and small enough to win.

332. Open your students' minds and value their opinions.

333. Value initiative, discourage imitation.

334. Encourage action, but value involvement.

335. Teach your students the value of unanswered questions.

336. Remember, not taking a position is taking a position.

337. Remind your students that strong points of view often are wrong.

338. Show your students the benefits in discovering new ways to think about old facts.

339. Teach that knowledge is good and ignorance is evil.

340. Show your students that an interest quotient is more valuable than an intelligence quotient.

341. Encourage action but value performance.

342. Value generosity; discourage jealousy.

343. Show your students the joy of doing what they think they cannot do.

344. Teach your students to finish what they start and not to start too much.

345. Remind yourself every day that simple thoughts often produce great discoveries.

346. Teach that achievement is based on information, motivation, and action.

347. Teach that knowledge is good and arrogance is evil.

348. Make only promises you plan to keep and keep those you make.

349. Teach your students that problems are opportunities for performance.

350. Teach your students that life is not a dress rehearsal.

351. Value getting the job done; encourage getting the job done right.

352. Listen more to what your students say than to how they say it.

353. Learn to accept even the smallest gift as if it was a long-cherished treasure.

354. Accept what has already taken place and try to make a difference in what hasn't.

355. Value curiosity, discourage deception.

356. Teach that persistence is good and ignorance is evil.

357. Encourage production but value imagination.

358. Teach your students to enjoy the process of learning.

359. Remember, the challenge of teaching is not in holding good cards but in playing well those you are dealt.

360. Make your classroom a haven where the benefits of examination are never distorted by the burdens of failure.

361. Teach your students that valuable lessons come in all sizes, shapes, and colors.

362. Accept tradition but value innovation.

363. Teach that confidence is good and arrogance is evil.

364. Value participation; discourage resistance.

365. Make teaching fun (write to me for ideas).

ICS BOOKS is offering YOU, the reader of this book the chance to have your own wisdom about teaching published sometime in the future.

Just send wisdom about teaching to:
ICS Books, Inc.
P.O. Box 10767
Merrillville, IN 46411-0767

Send a dated, typewritten copy of your wisdom with your name, address, and phone number. Include a permission line indicating that the submission(s) has (have) not been previously printed or published in any form, electronic or mechanical, including recorded broadcasts. Sign and date each submission.

ICS BOOKS will print your name somewhere in the book, stating you are the source of that wisdom.

ICS BOOKS reserves the right to edit or change your submission without your written permission.

If you would like some ideas for daily field trips (see item11) or ways to make teaching fun (see item 365), send a note and self-addressed, stamped envelope to ICS BOOKS. They will forward your request to me and I will send some more information to you.

Thanks for reading this book.

Bob Algozzine

Look for these other Little Books of Wisdom at your
favorite bookstore or outdoor retailer

Camping's Little Book of Wisdom
By Dave Scott
ISBN 0-934802-96-3 $5.95
&
Doctor's Little Book of Wisdom
By William W. Forgey, M.D.
ISBN 1-57034-016-1 $5.95

Look for Bachelor's and Traveler's Little Books of Wisdom
in the future